HOW THE ARMOR OF **GOD** PROTECTS THE SOUL OF MAN

RON FRANTZ

WESTBOW
PRESS
A DIVISION OF THOMAS NELSON

Unless otherwise noted, all Scripture quotations are from the New King James Version, Copyright 1982 by Thomas Nelson Inc.

WestBow Press books may be ordered through booksellers or by contacting:

WestBow Press
A Division of Thomas Nelson
1663 Liberty Drive
Bloomington, IN 47403
www.westbowpress.com
1-(866) 928-1240

ISBN: 978-1-4497-8955-8 (sc)
ISBN: 978-1-4497-8956-5 (e)

Library of Congress Control Number: 2013905511

Printed in the United States of America.

WestBow Press rev. date: 03/22/2013

Table of Contents

Acknowledgments

I THANKFULLY AND WHOLEHEARTEDLY ACKNOWLEDGE that everything I know and have written here I have been taught, either by the Holy Spirit or those led by the Holy Spirit. I do not believe that I have originated one thought (although I did originate this book) and am still seeking to learn more. I do, however, lay full claim to any mistakes or errors contained herein. There are still some things I can do on my own.

Preface

FOR MANY YEARS I HAVE listened to descriptions of the armor of God in various sermons and books and always came away with a sense of it being incomplete. Most of the material and references were to historical facts about armor used in the Roman era, and there seemed a continual bend to look at the armor from a natural standpoint.

I have sought the Lord diligently for an effective description and application that would help us to fight the good fight of faith and walk in authentic divine protection for the soul. The one point I believe many readers will discover is that they are already walking in various aspects of the armor, and having it articulated will help them increase its effectiveness.

Your Bible in your right hand and this book in the other is the way I intended this to work. I realize some in the body of Christ feel the need for things other than the Bible to increase their understanding. What *are* needed are things to increase our understanding of the Bible. The Lord helps us.

Ron Frantz

Chapter 1

Why Wear It

And there was war in Heaven!
(Revelation 12:7)

THE GREAT CONFLICT RAGING ON the earth today began countless millennia ago—in heaven! No one on the earth is immune or untouched! This discord is on the inside of us as well as in the outside realm in which we dwell.

> Where do wars and fights *come* from among you? Do *they* not *come* from your *desires for* pleasure that war in your members? (James 4:1 NKJV)

Willingly or unwillingly, we are in this battle because the only options we have been given are to be a victor or a victim! This conflict is between the reality and truth of God's Word and the alternate reality created through the lies and deception of Satan. The battleground of this conflict on earth is in the hearts and minds of men! Satan will do anything he can to distort the truth and undermine our faith in God's Word.

The main point and purpose of the conflict is to remove the Word of God from our hearts and prevent its fruit from being produced in our lives. Mark 4:17 tells us that affliction and persecution arise for *the Word's sake!* However, as the Word grows in our hearts, it will destroy the works of the Devil, just as it did when Jesus walked the earth. This is why the armor of God is so important!

The armor is the application of the Word of God to specific areas of our souls and is designed to defend and empower us during Satan's demonic attacks. Every piece of this armor is real and is very practical in our daily walks. It is not metaphorical, mystical, or mythical; it is real! There are six pieces of armor designed by God to protect our souls from the merciless and cruel Enemy who will exploit any weakness he can find in us. One of the most significant facts about the armor is that Jesus Himself, in His humanity, put it on.

> He saw that *there was* no man, And wondered that *there was* no intercessor; Therefore His own arm brought salvation for Him; And His own righteousness, it sustained Him. For He put on righteousness as a breastplate, And a helmet of salvation on His head; He put on the garments of vengeance for clothing, And was clad with zeal as a cloak. (Isaiah 59:15-17)

Our Father knew that Jesus would need heaven's armor to protect Himself as He entered into this vast conflict of mortal existence. If Jesus needed the armor for His time on earth, how much more do we? Our Father provided it for us because He knows what we are up against and what is coming our way in the future. He desires to protect us and prepare us for all of the challenges we must face as we do His will. We are not just getting armed so that we can fight; we are getting armed so we can *win!* God wants us to defeat the Enemy of our souls constantly, and since we are born of Him, victory is in our spiritual DNA. We are born winners! Even so, there is no victory without a fight. God is faithful; He will always preserve us and sustain us unto His kingdom, but to win victories for Him, we must have the offensive and defensive weapons that He has provided.

Prepare

Picture for a moment that you are watching a company of knights on horseback who are gathering on a medieval battlefield. They are gathering at the command of the king to defend his kingdom from an invading army. Lined up, the horses are stomping their hooves in anticipation of the charge. The banners are waving in the breeze as the sun glistens on all their armor. The signal is given, and as they charge bravely into battle, you notice in their midst one knight without any armor and wielding just a sword. Let us consider this knight who rushed into the battle without armor, disregarding the consequences. While we may admire his zeal and courage, in our minds we think, *There goes a casualty!*

Too many times I have witnessed new or untrained believers rushing out in their zeal to do all they can for God only to end up hurt or confused because of their vulnerability to the attacks of the Enemy. The best use for youthful zeal is to pursue with your whole heart a deeper relationship with God. Become rooted and grounded in Him! This alone will prepare and protect us!

Put on the Armor

How does this come about? How can we purposely put on each piece of armor and function in it at all times? The specific answers will come as we study each piece of the armor. However, in general, it begins with a decision! Each one of us must decide that the Word of God is absolutely true and completely trustworthy and make it the foundation of our faith.

The Most High God, Creator of heaven and earth, is big enough and wise enough to get to us exactly what He wants us to have. This understanding is foundational to the armor fully working in our lives because the armor is all about operating in the spiritual realities revealed and imparted to us through our covenant with God, which is revealed in His Word. We must know *Him* at least well enough to dispute the accusations that the Enemy is constantly making against God's character. These accusations are designed to undermine our faith in God's unchanging love for us and, if possible, make us feel unlovable. If he can, Satan and his demons will smack you in the head and then tell you it was God trying to get your attention. As we put on and activate the armor, the lies of the Enemy will be disarmed!

Perception: We Are at War!

The sooner we realize that the world around us is filled with demonic spirits that are trying to destroy our fellowship with God, the better equipped we will be. There is no great cause for fear or alarm, but it is a sobering reality. They are here to resist us. As we seek to wholeheartedly follow the Lord, we will encounter this resistance. The resistance is both external and internal. The more able we are to discern the source of the resistance, the quicker we will be able to neutralize it and move on. The external resistance is primarily from the demonic forces moving directly against us in whatever measure they can. The bombardment of our hearts and minds with thoughts and feelings of pride, jealousy, lusts, resentment, anger, bitterness, malice, discouragement, etc. are all designed to push us off the path of life and draw us into a mental warfare where Satan has a chance of winning, like he did with Eve.

Make no mistake: Satan's attack against us is in the mental arena; it is a psychological warfare, not a spiritual one. The Devil has been totally defeated in the spiritual realm and has been stripped of any and all spiritual armor and weaponry. Jesus was victorious on the cross and subjugated Satan and all his demonic hosts and held them captive. This is why we are directed in the Word to walk and live in the spirit, because there we have total victory over Satan, the flesh, the world, and all of the works of the Enemy. We will become confident in our warfare when we realize this one truth: the Devil has no armor, and that is why he attacks in the dark. He has no defense!

The weapons of our warfare are not carnal; they are powerful spiritual weapons and are mighty through God for pulling down every stronghold and casting down false imaginations. Satan's weapons are carnal. All that is in the world—the lust of the flesh, the lust of the eyes, and the pride of life—are his weapons. He feeds on the carnal nature of man, just as God told him in the garden of Eden that he would eat the dust of the earth. (Our flesh was formed out of the dust.) Satan is limited to what is common to man.

The concept that there is some great cosmic battle going on in the heavens between the forces of light and darkness is mostly a Hollywood idea. It may make a good movie theme, but it has no basis in reality. Satan would sure like us to think it is true; he really likes looking powerful. Is it possible that Satan and Hollywood have some kind of connection?

Indirectly, there is an external resistance that comes against us from the pressures of a society that is flowing in the opposite direction of God's design. It is when we turn our lives around to follow God and seek to do life His way that we really begin to experience this worldly current opposing us. This is why fellowship with other believers who are pressing in toward God is so important—because together it creates a flow in the right direction. If we try to overcome the flow of this worldly current on our own, we will soon become weary and begin to drift backward.

The internal resistance we often experience as we strive to follow the Lord is called "the flesh." This is the combination of thoughts, habits, and corrupted desires of our former way of life, and to whatever measure we continue to walk in the flesh, these same thoughts and habits are our current way of life. These "motions" of the flesh are still trapped in our physical bodies, and if we yield to them, they will take us in the wrong direction.

A main strategy of Satan against you is to "veil" his attacks with deceitful desires as he did with Eve. He attacked her relationship with

God by enticing her with a desire that could only be fulfilled if she directly disobeyed God's word. A major part of the war is discerning the truth from the lie! The truth is that God's Word operating in us fulfills all righteousness and goodness, which brings true personal fulfillment. The lie is that there can be fulfillment in our lives many other ways.

The armor of God is effective internally and externally during every attack. It defends against the external pressures and false perceptions that attempt to prevent us from fighting the good fight of faith. Internally, the armor has a tremendous stabilizing and purifying effect. Truth, righteousness, peace, faith, hope—all of these help provide an accurate perception of reality and keep us focused on what is important, which is winning the war.

Protection: We Are Vulnerable

Personal protection is one of the most fundamental reasons for wearing the armor. In many ways we are much more vulnerable than we care to admit. The thoughtless actions or hurtful words of others often wound us deeply enough to affect our attitude and hinder our relationships with God and others. The sheer number of wounded Christians (inside and outside of church) is evidence enough of how desperately we need protection. Without armor, our hearts and minds are dangerously vulnerable to even the most basic attacks. Consequently, most churches resemble a crisis intervention center more than a spiritual growth center. This isn't meant as a criticism, but we must understand why things are the way they are in order to create effective change. Remaining vulnerable only sets us up as a target and will perpetuate the attitude of survival Christianity. This attitude will quickly change once we are clothed with God's protection and power, and our victories will become much more frequent and attainable. Better yet, when we gain ground, we will be able to keep it and maintain our spiritual progress.

Provision: Supernatural Ability

The spirit armor is God's provision for us to be supernaturally able to withstand and overcome *every* attack of the enemy! Remember our opening declaration: this war began in heaven, and it was won in heaven. Knowing this will help us understand the complete necessity of using heaven's weapons to *personally* gain heaven's victory in every area of our lives. All else is futile; there is no other way to win. If there was another way we would have found it by now.

Man has tried everything, from self-exaltation to self-abasement, from meditation to mysticism. Plans, programs, and various political systems have all been tried repeatedly and failed. Even religion (which at one time or another has embraced all the above), ardently and sincerely exercised by countless thousands, has only managed to produce a hollow echo of the victory that God has for us in Christ Jesus. We know this in our hearts, so let us forsake the futility of natural means and worldly wisdom by embracing the grace of heaven's provision for complete victory: the armor of God.

Preparation: Equipped for Conflict

Why should we take the time to put on and wear the armor of God before we need it? The answer is obvious, but often unheeded. You can't get armed in the middle of a fight; there isn't time. Plus, trying get armed in the middle of a battle is the wrong activity in which to be involved. We will need to be fighting and focusing on our enemy, not on ourselves. Another important reason is that when we are distracted or ineffective in a battle, we create a gap in the ranks. Our family and our brothers and sisters close to us may become more exposed to an attack by our ineffectiveness. This happens way more often than we realize. It is strategically necessary that we be fully armed and prepared for these spiritual conflicts that the Word of God assures us will certainly come, not just for our safety, but also for those close to us.

Above all else, our God says to put it on! This is not a suggestion; it is a directive from the One who sees the end from the beginning. If we refuse this wisdom from above there is no doubt that we will suffer needlessly from the attacks of the enemy. The armor is a glorious impartation of God's grace; it is a generous gift. We must not forfeit this grace through a lack of preparation.

Purpose: Victory Depends on It

The bottom-line reason for wearing the armor is that our victory depends on it! Without the armor we will lose again and again, simply because we are not equipped to successfully stand against the wiles of the Devil. This is not to say that we won't make it to heaven, but we will fail to fulfill our purpose while we are here on earth. I have noticed a strong tendency in Christians who are not equipped for warfare. They will avoid spiritual conflict at almost any cost because they know they are not ready to deal with it. Even if they wanted to deal with it they wouldn't have the supernatural ability to do so. Consequently, there are fear issues that creep in due to a sense vulnerability to reprisals and attacks from the enemy if they take a bold, strong stand against his actions. Satan is going to attack anyway, so you might as well make the attack count for something and gain the benefits God has promised.

The Word also promises that God will not allow you to be tempted beyond what you are able to deal with! Did you grasp that? It said *able*. God is saying that with His protection and help we *are* able to take that step and make our stand. As we take that step and get our armor on, all of the promises of being an overcomer become available to us. *Praise God!*

In the Revelation 2 and 3, the Lord said,

> To him who overcomes I will give to eat from the tree of
> life, he shall not be hurt by the second death, I will give
> him some hidden manna, I will give him power over the
> nations, I will confess his name before My Father and
> before His angels, I will make him a pillar in the temple,
> I will grant him to sit with Me on My throne.

To inherit these promises we must overcome our enemies. So let's get armed! Our victory depends on it!

Chapter 2

What Are We Protecting?

ALTHOUGH THIS INFORMATION MAY BE redundant to many, a brief description of how we were created is necessary to know exactly what we are protecting and why.

> [A]nd may your whole spirit, soul and body be preserved
> blameless. (1 Thessalonians 5:23)

These are the three main dimensions of our being. First and foremost is the spirit of man. Our Lord Jesus, in His classic teaching on salvation said, "that which is born of flesh is flesh, and that which is born of spirit is spirit" (John 3:6). We all have earthly fathers of our flesh. When we are born again of the spirit, God Himself is the Father of our spirit (Hebrews 12:9). This is the new man, the new creation created in God's image and likeness.

Man is also a living soul. The soul of man is our individuality, our persona. God has made us all unique for a purpose. He enjoys our individuality (Psalm 33:15). All of this is contained in a limited physical body for identification and location.

Isaiah 43:7 speaks of man's being this way: "Whom I have created for My glory, I have formed him, yes, I have made him." God created our spirit for His glory! He formed our bodies out of the dust of the earth, and He made our souls for His pleasure. There are many different dimensions to the spirit and many different complexities to our body, but for now we will focus on the soul of man. This is what we are protecting with the armor of God.

The three main areas of the soul are the mind (what we think), the will (what we choose), and the emotions (what we feel).

The Mind: What We Think

Our mind is the arena of our reflective thought and consciousness. It is set in our being as the place of awareness and self-determination. This is the way God made us, and it is most precious to Him. God loves us individually and cherishes our individual expressions of love and faith. How important are our thoughts, especially what we think about God? It is amazing how life altering our thoughts can be, and how powerfully they affect our perceptions and views of the world around us. When Satan was able to implant one false thought into Eve's mind, it totally altered her perception of the Tree of Knowledge of Good and Evil. In light of this new information, she began to view it as something desirable. What changed? Her view of the tree was no longer based on the truth of God's word; it became based on a deceptive lie, which introduced a whole different series of thought patterns.

Romans 12:2 gives insight and instruction on where to focus our thinking, which is so needed for this information age in which we live. We must guard our thoughts from the profusion of information that seeks to conform us to the world's way of thinking. We do this by the transforming power of holy knowledge—revelatory knowledge of the will of God. Conformity and agreement with the world's thoughts will always produce worldly results. Our thinking should be constantly going through transformation by renewing our mind with spiritual information. As we come into holy agreement (on whatever level we are able) with God's revelation about who He really is and who we really are, it will literally change our view of what is actually going on around us every day.

Nowhere is this understanding more important than in our spiritual warfare. We must allow the spiritual information in the Word of God to transform our thinking of how we can overcome every attack of the Enemy and walk in victory. The Word tells us how to fight. Even though the attack is against our mind, we are not fighting with mental weapons. When Satan attacks our mind with thoughts and feelings of fear, doubt, worry, or lust, we do not fight back with thoughts of refusal. Neither should we try to block these thoughts out or switch our thinking to something else. We are to fight against the attacks of Satan on our mind with spiritual words and actions!

You can't fight thoughts with thoughts; this is where so many lose their victory. The Word says we overcome by the blood of the Lamb and the word of our testimony. The Lord said that when He returns He will fight against His enemies with the sword of His mouth—meaning His words. Over and over again words are described as swords and arrows; they are our weaponry.

The next time thoughts of fear and doubt attack you, speak the Word to them. If worry or lust comes against your mind, speak God's thoughts to it and see what happens. His words spoken through your lips in faith will have the same effect on the Devil as if He spoke them. Of course, to speak the Word you have to know the Word, which brings us back to Romans 12:2 and renewing our understanding to be spiritually minded. And how do we become spiritually minded? Simply by filling the content of our mind with spiritual things. It's a choice.

The Will: What We Choose

With the freedom to think comes the freedom to choose. I suppose if God had wanted to He could have made us unable to make our own choices so that the only option we had was to do His will. But without the power of choice, how could we choose to love Him?

How could we willingly obey and serve Him? How could we seek Him and delight in discovering more things about Him without the ability to seek other things? It is obvious that a willing love is the only kind that would satisfy His heart—and ours. Our heavenly Father created us to be passionate and wholehearted so that we could make the glorious decision to desire *Him* above all else.

A great contrast in Scripture and history is the tremendous lengths God is willing to go in order to protect our free will, as opposed to Satan's attempts to continually dominate or destroy it! Any action or system that seeks to eliminate or control man's free will is satanic in nature and will always produce bondage and destruction. This is not to say that anyone can do whatever he or she will to do. Our choices always have consequences, and the law of sowing and reaping is a reality we all face. If we choose to sow to the flesh, we will reap corruption. If we choose to sow to the spirit, we will reap eternal life. In the days of Moses, God said to Israel, "See, I have set before you life and death, blessing and cursing. Choose life that you may live." The underlying principle in both of these is that we get to choose what we sow, because without the power of choice, we cannot grow and mature as sons and daughters of God.

So, in conclusion, Satan is always seeking ways to manipulate or divert our will from being in line with God's will. His schemes and deceitful temptations are designed to cause us to make the wrong choices and draw us away from the path of life. To defeat this, the Word of God must be the foundation of our thinking and our choosing. When acted on, the truth will always set us free!

The Emotions: What We Feel

Our emotions have a tremendous capacity to be affected by all three realms of existence—spirit, soul, and body. This is also by God's design. He created us to feel as He feels! When spiritual realities touch our emotions, the effects can be very intense and run deep into our being. After Jesus talked with two of His disciples on the road to Emmaus, they exclaimed to each other, "Did not our hearts burn within us while He talked with us?" A burning heart and a passionate desire for God are meant to be the experience of all His disciples.

Our thoughts and our choices will also directly affect how we feel. Most of the time, our emotions have no other basis in reality other than what we think. How many times do we stimulate strong emotions simply by thinking about situations and circumstances in our lives? For me, daily! Also, I am sure that we are all aware of how easily our emotions are affected by our physical surroundings and experiences. This is why they are so often the target of the Enemy's attacks.

Our emotions are the most vulnerable part of our souls. They must be well guarded from destructive influences such as jealousy, envy, hate, etc. Most of this will be taken care of when we renew our minds with the truth and align our will with God's will, but there are almost always some areas in our emotional chemistry where we will need some healing and cleansing, especially in the area of emotional memories. The good news is that the Word of God has an unlimited ability to heal and sanctify our emotions and even to change our emotional chemistry to more closely match His. The Holy Spirit will definitely lead us in this process, for He is our sanctifier. We need to have our emotions sanctified in order for our souls to be stable and function properly.

Unhealthy, damaging emotions must be submitted to the power and authority of the Word of God. Most of the time this will involve forgiving what someone has said or done to us or receiving forgiveness for what we have done, but it also includes other things, like fears that are caused by traumatic events or lies about God that warp our emotional well-being. Whatever the case may be, God's grace is sufficient to bring us real emotional restoration. The benefit of healthy emotions (besides simply feeling good) is they provide a great source of strength and motivation for spiritual advancement.

The primary function of our emotional makeup is to make us responsive and give us emotional energy and motivation to do all of the things that we know in our hearts we should be doing. From a natural standpoint, it is amazing how often people will rely on emotional motivation to actually do something. Even though we know we have to do it, whatever it is, so many times we put it off until we "feel" like doing it—in other words, until we have adequate emotional strength. The same is often true for prayer and reading the Bible, and although we as believers must not rely on just emotional energy to do what is right, it sure is nice to have it. It is always good to be zealously affected by a good thing.

How do we increase our emotional energy for spiritual activities? Whatever we focus our attention on generally receives the bulk of our emotional energy, so first, gain information in the area you want your increase. If you are sensing in your heart that you need to pray more, get accurate, powerful books on prayer and feed on them. When you have enough light and information to make an informed decision, decide on a prayer strategy and how much time you want to devote to daily prayer. Then make a bold declaration to God, to yourself, and to the Devil of what you decide. Look in the mirror and declare to yourself what you are going to do—with God's help and power! Say it out loud, and be loud about it. Continue to do this even if you have setbacks and encounter resistance (and you will). Make the declaration and continue toward your goal, and behold, great emotional energy will be released through your decision and declaration.

The Human Heart: What We Believe

Undergirding all three areas of our souls is something most important: what we fundamentally believe. What we think may change quickly with new information. What we choose may vary from day to day. Our emotions can be a virtual rollercoaster. But what we really believe in the depths of our hearts is not so easily changed.

I have included the heart in this discussion of what we are protecting because it is the place of real power working in our lives, and it is the *ultimate* target of the enemy! Proverbs 4:23 says, "Keep your heart with all diligence, for out of it spring the issues of life." Our minds, wills, and emotions are the point of attack, but the heart is always the main objective. Our Lord Jesus tried to explain to the disciples that it was not what went in to their bodies that defiled them, but what came out of their hearts. He declared, "Out of the heart proceeds . . ." From our hearts flows the powerful forces that fundamentally affect our lives. This is how we received our salvation from the Lord: we believe it in our hearts, and we say it with our mouths. So, by protecting our souls with the armor of God, we are also keeping our hearts from destructive influences.

The Heart Defined

I have heard many say that the heart of man is his soul. Others have said it is his spirit. But in the Word it is given attributes of both the soul and spirit. The Word is the one thing that can distinguish between the spirit and the soul and can accurately define the heart, as stated in Hebrews 4:12.

> For the Word of God is living and powerful, sharper than
> any two edged sword, piercing even to the division of soul
> and spirit, and is a discerner of the thoughts and intents
> of the heart.

The heart of man is the place in our beings where the spirit and soul connect, much in the same way our brains and bodies are connected physically. The hundreds of nerves and nerve endings that culminate in the brain produce a sensory input to the body. If these nerves in one part of our body are damaged, that part becomes unresponsive. This can also happen to our hearts. Cruel, damaging words or experiences can cause our hearts to become unresponsive and hard, especially over time. Proverbs 15:4 describes it this way: "A wholesome tongue is a tree of life, but perverseness in it breaks the spirit."

When areas of our heart connections get "broken," our souls (mind, will, emotions) are not able to receive proper spiritual input and so become darkened and deadened. The longer this continues, the greater the disconnection becomes, to the point that it would take a miracle to fully restore the heart. I can say this from experience! This is where anointed preaching and teaching comes in. These wholesome, life-filled words bring restoration and healing.

One of the things restored is the conscience. The conscience is the voice of our hearts, and when restored will speak to us with deep conviction about the issues of life. It is the blending together of the truth that we intuitively know in our spirit combined with the knowledge and understanding gained through our life experiences. These convictions come out of this combined knowledge of our souls and spirits (the literal translation for the word *conscience* in the New Testament is *co-knowledge*), declaring to us what is morally right and true. It is set in our beings as a moral guide and judge. This is another reason why feeding our souls with accurate, true knowledge is so important. It will help the voices of our consciences be clear and strong, which enables us to have a more effortless cooperation with the spirit and defeat the condemnation that Satan is constantly attempting to put on us.

This is a most important point. A God-ordained activity of our hearts is to convict us when we do wrong. It is the Holy Spirit working with us, convicting us of the truth. The adversary will try to get involved in this same activity and accuse us of being sinful in order to condemn us. Satan loves to pass himself off as the Holy Spirit and try to declare to us that we are unworthy and undesirable to God. This *must* be defeated!

We must be rock solid on the difference between conviction and condemnation, or we will always be vulnerable. The truth is that the Holy Spirit *never* condones sin, but when we err from the truth, He deals with it and will continue to deal with it until it is totally dealt with. Whatever we have done, the Holy Spirit leads us specifically to own up to it, make confession, ask for forgiveness, and receive cleansing. He then works with us to restore our lives so that this sin no longer has any place in us while always maintaining the goal of victory and redemption. Further more, the Holy Spirit *never* condemns us or judges us. He simply speaks the unchanging truth in love and gives us grace to overcome. On the other hand, as you know, Satan will accuse us to our own hearts and attempt to condemn us as a hopeless hypocrite for sinning. He will say, "You might as well face reality. You know how you are, and God knows it also. You did it and you will probably do it again, so what is the use of trying to be something that you are not?"

The Devil is a liar! There is no condemnation to those who are in Christ. Jesus won't condemn us, and the Devil can't. In reality, my sin is none of the Devil's business. Jesus is the one who paid my debt and redeemed me. So if I sin, it is dealt with between my Lord and me and whomever I may have sinned against.

One time the Devil was trying to bother me about a mistake I had made (and repented of) and this Scripture came to my mind: "Let the redeemed of the Lord say *so*." Now I was ready, and when that demon brought it up again, I said to it out loud, "So? It's none of your business. Jesus is my Lord." The Devil left!

Chapter 3

Preamble to the Armor

Finally, my brethren, be strong in the Lord
and in the power of His might.
Ephesians 6:10

IN ORDER TO UNLOCK AND reveal the staggering grace and implications of this verse we must delve a little deeper into the translation of these three words from the Greek text: *strong*, *power*, and *might*. The reason a deeper meaning is necessary for these three words as used in our text is that in the KJV (and most other translations) they are interchangeable, but in the Greek text it is not so.

Fortunately, there are many awesome commentaries and so much good information available today to help us increase our knowledge and gain a clearer understanding of this subject. I encourage you, as you read, to make full use of all the scholarly resources you have available so as to make this verse come alive.

Dunamis: Power

The actual Greek word for *strong* in the text is *endunamis*, which is a strengthened form of the root word *dunamis*. This word has received a lot of exposure in the body of Christ through expository teaching and preaching with the definition of being the explosive, creative power of God, which is true. We get our English words *dynamo* and *dynamite* from the Greek word *dunamis*, which also implies inherent, self-energizing, raw power. It is used in Acts 1:8 by the Lord to describe the glorious power that His disciples were soon to experience: "You shall receive POWER [dunamis] when the Holy Ghost is come upon you."

The significance to this meaning in the text is that we are to be "*endunamis* [empowered] in the Lord." This same energizing, glorious power is working in us for victory in our warfare, but it is only available to us "in the Lord." It is in Him, not in me. God alone is the source of this creative, explosive power, and desires us to have it working in our lives to accomplish all that He wants done. Every instruction God gives us has in it the grace and wisdom necessary to fulfill it when we embrace it with simple trust and obedience. It is through the *lordship* of Jesus working in my life that this tremendous power can be released. I am empowered in the Lord!

Kratos: Force

This Greek word, translated as *power* in our text, is translated other times as *might* or *strength*, and implies the force exerted in the demonstration of God's power. By analogy, when dynamite explodes and releases power, a force is created that affects everything in the immediate vicinity, depending on the degree of power of the dynamite. This is a good description of kratos. It is the force released when God's power is exercised and in operation.

As an example, let's look at the use of *kratos* in Luke 1:51: "He has shown strength [kratos] with His arm." The action of this verse is God demonstrating by force the strength of His arm against the proud and mighty in the earth. Similarly, in weightlifting, a person demonstrates how much force [kratos] they can apply to the weights as they lift them, and the amount of force being exerted is measured by how many pounds of steel are lifted. This measurement expresses a person's "ability."

Ischus: Ability

Our ability reveals what we can actually do. It is the end result accomplished by the force we exert. This is a good description of the meaning of *ischus* (the word translated as *might* in our text). If I lift with all my might and can get two hundred pounds up over my head, it is an accurate measure of my ability to do so. Yet, more than strength alone, my ability to lift the weights is increased by practice, technique, and the knowledge of how to lift. All of these factors combined are the measure of my ability. To sum it all up from this natural standpoint, when exerted, the power (dunamis) in my muscles releases force (kratos) to lift, which reveals my measurable ability (ischus).

Back to our text of Ephesians 6:10. What about God's power? What kind of power are we talking about? It is inexhaustible, never-ending, matchless power! How great is the force His power can generate? It is an irresistible, unstoppable force! What is the measure of His ability? His is a limitless, incalculable, all-encompassing ability!

This is what we are being called to, in Him. This is the level of grace that we are being admonished to receive for our warfare! Glory to God! So, in modern terms, an expanded version of our text may read, "Finally my brethren, be fully empowered in the Lord, and in the irresistible force of His limitless ability."

The Whole Armor

Ephesians 6:11 says, "Put on the whole armor of God, that you may be able to stand." At this point, it is good to reiterate that the armor of God is designed to protect our souls and recognize that the whole armor is needed to be fully protected. This admonition is repeated in verse thirteen for emphasis: the whole armor is necessary to stand successfully in our warfare.

There is a tendency in the church to stop short of receiving and walking in all that God has for us. We get one or two good things, feel satisfied with our attainment, and quit pursuing. This will not work with the armor. To obtain only three or four pieces and somehow feel that we are adequately protected is a dangerous error that will cost us later on. The goal of this writing is to get everyone fully equipped, with every piece of armor working at least in some measure. Then, as you stand your ground you will become more and more skillful in the weapons of your warfare, to the point that some of the attacks of the enemy, which in times past would have had a very damaging effect, will barely leave a mark!

It is the whole armor that gives us this divine empowerment and provision to successfully stand our ground against the schemes of the Devil. This is the first level of victory: simply being able to stand our ground without wavering. The Enemy of our souls is constantly scheming and devising ways to get us to compromise our stance on the Word of God, on who we are in Christ, and on enforcing his inevitable defeat. All of these schemes, these wiles of the devil, have a singular purpose: to bring our minds, wills, and emotions back under the influence and control of the kingdom of darkness. What we think, what we choose, what we feel and desire—these are the primary targets of the principalities and powers that we wrestle against. Some translations say "rulers and authorities" instead of "principalities and powers," which is more understandable in today's terminology. Demonic spirits are constantly seeking ways to gain authority over our lives and attempting to rule over us with pressure tactics and deceptive traps, *all* of which require our consent to work.

This is such a *key* revelation! The Devil cannot make us do anything. Sin no longer has dominion over us. It must have our consent on some level to be able to have any control in our lives. Breaking these areas of agreement is a major strategy to getting free from any bondages or addictions that we may struggle with. It is the first step. For instance, as a young Christian I struggled with a bondage to cigarettes. It was a mental and physical addiction that I knew in my heart I must overcome. I would try to quit, but in my thoughts and words I would still agree with the addiction and say things like "It's too hard to quit" and "I don't think I can do it"—or compromise and say, "It's okay in moderation." In all of this I was agreeing with the enemy that I was defeated, and the problem was, it was a fact. I was defeated. But facts can change!

When it got through to me that my Lord Jesus had already bought and paid for my victory, and if I came into agreement with Him and accepted it by faith, then I would have access to His supernatural ability and authority to overcome everything and change the facts. It happened. I broke agreement with the Enemy and verbally agreed with God that He had set me free. The struggling didn't immediately stop, but instead of struggling with smoking, I was struggling toward freedom from smoking, which happened a few weeks later.

As we seek to grow in the Lord we will all encounter the various struggles and trials of our faith. During these times, especially in times of intense struggle, we must guard our hearts against that favorite weapon of the enemy: *condemnation*. Satan will do everything he can to create an area of struggling in our lives and will then bombard us with thoughts of how weak and hypocritical we are for struggling. Here is where the armor goes to work! Struggling with sin issues does not make any believer a hypocrite. The "you're not perfect, so you are a hypocrite" attack is a deceptive lie from the Enemy thrown at you to destroy your confidence in God's love and weaken your faith. The truth is, the very fact that we are still struggling to please God is proof that we want to be free. Otherwise, why would we struggle?

Here is another truth: condemnation is *never* from God! There is no condemnation to those who are in Christ. Any thoughts of condemnation or feelings of unworthiness are all outside of Christ and are not an expression of His heart in any way. As a believer, you are a person of destiny who wants to love God more even though you may currently struggle with things that get in the way of your destiny. Our identities must be rooted in the truth and in our future, in God's eternal purpose for us, not in our past or present failures.

I admonish you as a brother, however, to be cautious here. As I stated earlier, do not confuse conviction with condemnation. Conviction is the great blessing of the Holy Spirit, convincing us of the truth. Holy-Spirit conviction of the truth is very valuable in identifying any areas of agreement with the Enemy. In conviction, we will have that strong inner sense that something is not right with whatever we just said, did, or even thought. Take heed to these promptings of the Spirit. Pray, find out what the Word has to say, and ask God to reveal what is going on. Conviction brings victory; condemnation brings defeat.

The Evil Day

> . . . that you may be able to withstand in the evil day.
> Ephesians 6:13

As we take our stand and press in to God's purposes for us, there will be days of concentrated demonic attacks, when it seems like all hell is breaking loose against you. It may be coming at you from all directions at a level you have never experienced before. It may even seem hopeless, but whatever you do, don't back off from the Word of God. This is when we will be doing "all" we can just to stand and not give up or run away. Now is when being strong in the Lord and in the power of *His* might is so glorious and effective. Maximize your dependence on the Lord, verbally roll your cares over on Him, and above all else, simply stand your ground.

What we cannot allow to happen at this point is a bunch of unfocused questioning, like "Why is this happening?," "What am I going to do now?," or "Will this ever end?" If we let our minds become available to a lot of questioning, the Devil (and others) will supply us with all kinds of answers. Our best strategy for the "evil day" is to trust in the Lord with all of our hearts and not to lean on our own understanding of the situation. Simply trust. God is still God, no matter what. This situation didn't catch Him off guard or dethrone Him. Keep doing whatever God has given you to do and let Him work in you.

Paul and Silas are prime examples of this. In the book of Acts, by a vision from the Lord, they were called to the city of Philippi to preach the gospel. A short time later they were being beaten with rods and thrown into the inner dungeon in that city. So here they are, beaten and bloody, their feet in stocks, with no outward hope of help or justice. Who knows what thoughts may have assailed their minds? But God was still God to them, whatever the circumstances. So they just stood their ground, began to praise the Lord, and exalted Him as God over their circumstances, and the circumstances dramatically changed. They were set free and many people were saved.

It is good to remember that tests and trials have a time limit, and since we are going to live forever, time is on our side. Be willing to have a patient faith that can outlast the circumstances. Being empowered to hold our ground is vitally important to our spiritual growth and our advancement. We do *not* want to get caught up in the cycle of regaining the same ground over and over. This constant advancing and retreating may make us seem busy, but in reality it is an indication that we are letting our armor down and losing ground somewhere. Seek to win in the real issues.

I would also encourage you to look for the benefits of being attacked. These periods of concentrated warfare will definitely reveal any vulnerable or unguarded areas in your soul. Don't go through attacks without learning something! I realize this may not sound appealing, but it is wise, and will make winning easier. Being able to consistently win is a huge benefit, because victory always brings promotion in the kingdom of God. Goliath's defeat made David an overnight success and set him on course to fulfill his destiny.

In conclusion I add a word of encouragement. When we fully accomplish Ephesians 6:13, and we have on the whole armor so that we can withstand attacks, we will experience a glorious reality. Many of the darts that are fired at us by the Enemy that would have been devastating before will hit the armor and be absorbed rather than hitting and wounding us. Instead of being excruciating, we will find to our amazement that the blows we are dealt in life will become stimulating encouragements to fight the good fight of faith. This will also affect our prayer focus. Instead of spending our time praying for the healing of all the wounds we have, we can pray for those people who were used by Satan to try to hurt us. We will be able to go on the offensive for them as well.

Chapter 4

The Armor

As we examine the individual pieces of the armor, it is important to note that the first three are characterized and preceded by the word *having*, putting the nonauxiliary verb in the past tense—"having girded your loins," "having put on the breastplate," and "having shod your feet." This implies that the function of these first three pieces of armor is constant and foundational to protecting our position. These realities must be in place and functioning *before* the conflict.

The second three pieces are operational, and are characterized with *taking*—taking the shield, taking the helmet, and taking the sword. *Taking* implies the present tense, which means these three pieces are operated during each conflict. This "having" and "taking" aspects will be clearer as we see how each piece functions.

Loins Girded

Loins as used in the Word speaks of the creative, reproductive aspect of man. For example, in Hebrews 7:10, it states that Levi (Abraham's great grandson) was still in the "loins" of Abraham when Melchizedek met him, which simply implies that he had not yet been born. It is the same word used for *loins* in Ephesians 6:14, where it indicates reproductive ability, though some versions inaccurately say "your waist."

This prompts the question: what is that creative, reproductive part of our souls that we are protecting with the truth? *Our imaginations*—the capacity that was given to us by God for creative thinking! The imagination is a very powerful force, especially when the Spirit of God is inspiring it. The imagination has given birth to all manner of inventions, buildings, art, music, etc. It is capable of creating breathtaking beauty, solving seemingly impossible problems, and expanding beyond any physical limitations. Man imagined flying for centuries before he could get off the ground, and then it happened. Once he could get off the ground he began to imagine flying to the moon and beyond.

This part of the soul has such limitless capacity for growth and change, for good or evil, which is why it must be thoroughly guarded. When the imagination of man became *inspired by sin*, it gave birth to all manner of evil on the earth. In the book of Genesis, the first civilization came to the point everyone's imagination was only ever evil. Think of it: this evil had so totally infected the collective imagination of the race of man that it threatened the destiny of the whole planet. So God intervened and saved the only righteous man and his family, but had to allow the rest of mankind to be destroyed by the flood. In Genesis 11:6 the Lord made an observation that when the people began to operate in their collective imagination, nothing would be impossible to them. So He confused their language.

First Peter 1:13 describes the donning of the first piece of armor this way: "gird up the loins of your mind and be sober." Letting our imaginations run wild can be intoxicating, but we are cautioned not to let this happen. Our imaginations need the boundaries of the Word of God to be guarded from being led astray into the wilderness of unsanctified thoughts and emotions. We want to keep a strong grip on reality so that false, unproductive concepts don't end up dominating our thinking.

This is clearly seen in the original temptation, described in Genesis 3:1-7. In verse one, the serpent begins covertly questioning what God said by putting it in a negative context: "Has God said, 'You shall NOT eat of every tree'?," clearly misquoting God's words to Eve. This was done to draw her mentally into a dialogue about what God really meant. Eve responds with the proper information and even gives the judgment for disobedience: "lest you die." Next the serpent openly defies the judgment and says, "You will not surely die," in essence saying that God lied to Eve. Now, here is the main point: to make his lie believable, Satan gives Eve an ulterior motive to why God said, "You shall surely die." He attacked God's character, which shook Eve's faith! Satan's reasoning was this: "God doesn't want you to know what He knows so that you will stay dependent on Him. God is holding out on you, Eve, so that He can control you. God knows if you eat this fruit you can be like Him and decide for yourself what is good or evil." This is an all-out attack on the very nature and person of God, and Eve was apparently vulnerable to this attack. This new line of reasoning captured her imagination, and so, infected with this new (false) information, she takes the first step into sin. She reexamines this tree in the light of this new reasoning and falls completely into the world of temptation described in 1 John 2:16: "For all that is in the world, the lust of the flesh, the lust of the eyes and the pride of life."

Eve looked at the tree with her new perspective and saw that, in her opinion, it was good for food—she was experiencing the lust of the flesh. How did she know it was good for food if she had never tasted it? She *imagined* it was good! Then she discovered it was pleasant to the eyes (thus she felt the lust of the eyes). Last of all, she determined that it was a tree to be desired, to make her wise (she felt the pride of life). So, filled with thoughts of her own personal fulfillment, she chose to eat—*and lost*. We all face the same challenge.

All of us have tasted this fruit "for all have sinned and fall short of the glory"—*except one*!

Just as the attack is clearly seen in the original temptation, the answer is clearly seen in the original victory of Luke 4:1-13. Jesus was attacked with the same temptations under extremely severe circumstances, but with different results. Satan first tempted Jesus to use his power to fulfill His own personal appetite (i.e., Satan tempted Him with the lust of the flesh). Jesus, however, refused to be pulled in to a personal dialogue with Satan. He answered the temptation with "It is written." He blasted Satan's attack with a specific, direct application of the Word of God (as we will see later, this is the shield of faith in operation). Satan then proceeded to show Jesus what all He could have if He would bow to temptation, the world and all of its glory (i.e., to the lust of the eyes). Jesus responded with "It is written." Last of all, the Devil asked Him to prove something (i.e., he tried to activate His pride of life). This temptation was very crafty because Satan used a promise of Scripture, hoping to lure Jesus into testing God. Jesus simply responded with the Word and won a complete victory.

Jesus knew it was not up to man to create situations in order to prove whether God's Word is true. No situation or circumstance can judge the validity of God's Word. The only way to prevent this is to have our loins (creative abilities) girded and surrounded with the truth. The truth, you know, will not only make you free—it will keep you free. However, I have frequently seen one paradox concerning the application of the truth to our lives. Although the truth is infinitely powerful to set our souls free, most of the time it will make our flesh very uncomfortable, even to the point of feeling crucified. If we have not crucified and do not crucify the flesh ourselves, on purpose, we will not be capable of fully embracing the truth in such a way that it can keep us free. But if we truly decide to deny ourselves and take up our crosses and follow Him, the truth becomes glorious, sweet to the taste, and passionately desired. It will propel us into the liberty of being the sons and daughters of God.

What Is Truth?

There are two different aspects to reality: temporal and eternal. Truth is eternal reality! It is as unalterable and unchangeable as is God. Jesus said it best in John 17:17: "Sanctify them through Your truth. Your Word is truth." Specifically, truth is the eternal reality expressed and revealed in God's Word.

Having the activity of our imagination surrounded and guarded with the truth of this Word will sanctify our souls from the onslaught of lies and deceptions that are so prevalent in this temporal reality. Temporal reality is just that. It is real, but it is temporary. Many Eastern religions and even some "Christian" ones have tried to mysticize this by saying that the temporal, physical world is not actually real. They claim that the physical limitations, pain, and suffering are all illusions, which they seek to escape via an elaborate series of mental gymnastics and disciplines.

Hogwash! The present physical limitations are real, and they were created by God. All of the pain and suffering was added later by man through union with sin and Satan but are still an intrinsic part of this present reality, and we have to deal with it. To deny their reality will short-circuit our faith and make us ineffective in overcoming these temporary realities with the eternal reality of God's Word, which is the whole point of our being here.

Romans 8:18-22 reveals that we were subjected to the futility of a limited mortal existence for certain reasons, one of which is to learn how to properly handle freedom and spiritual power in the middle of all of our mistakes. Mistakes made in a temporal setting are temporary and very changeable, and we can quickly grow beyond them. But when Satan created iniquity in eternity, his consequences and judgment were eternal. I thank God for where we are!

So, the first piece of armor is our creative imagination, surrounded and held steady with the truth. This will give our souls balance and composure in the midst of conflict and will protect our minds from building false concepts of reality. It will also defend us against the ungodly forces of falsehood, hypocrisy, and the spirit of error. The truth is also a great defense against the spirit of false prophecy. Demons love to talk to us as if they were sent from God; this is a spirit of false prophecy. When you know the truth it is easy to spot these false messages, because they will not line up with the Word. They usually will be either self-exalting or self-debasing, or simply appeal to our natural desires. The two tests for false prophecy or true prophecy are always the same: does it line up with the Word, and does the Holy Spirit give a witness to it in my heart?

Imagine God's Word! It is truly the Spirit of prophecy. Turn your creativity loose on what your life would look like if the promises in God's word were fulfilled in you, exactly as they are written! This is where we are headed. Having our imaginations surrounded with truth will also eliminate so much of the spiritual fantasizing that goes on in the church. We would not allow scenarios to build up in our mind, like how awesome our churches ministries would be if we were in charge, or how wonderful life would be if we were married to this person or that person. If we allow such thoughts to grow in us they will quickly affect our attitudes and actions in a very negative way. Don' let yourself go there! Loving the truth and embracing God's purposes for us will always be more fruitful and fulfilling than anything we can dream up.

Summary of Our Loins Girded with Truth

Loins are the creative, reproductive area of the soul, our imagination.

Girded means encompassed and surrounded by and focused on the truth.

The *truth* is God's eternal reality expressed and revealed in His Word.

- This piece of armor gives the soul balance and composure in battle and doesn't allow the imagination to build false concepts of reality.

- The armor of truth exposes and defends against falsehood, hypocrisy, and the spirit of error. This armor will also guard us against the spirit of false prophecy.

The Breastplate

The root word of *imagination* is *image*. We were created and are recreated in the image of God. The inner image we have of ourselves overwhelmingly influences our identity and goes to the core of who we are. The breastplate of righteousness protects this area that is vital for boldness and confidence in God, our new identities in Christ.

From a natural standpoint, our identities are based primarily on our own ideas about ourselves. These ideas can be influenced by family, friends, occupation, and culture, but ultimately it is our personal ideas about who and what we are that establish our core identity. After we are born again and recreated in God's image we begin the process of basing our identity on what God says about us, through receiving His ideas and intention for us. He created us for His glorious, eternal purposes and has total confidence in our ability to do all His good pleasure in Christ. This new-creation identity (i.e., seeing myself as God sees me), is fundamentally accomplished by removing of one thing and replacing it with another. We must allow the truth to remove from us a sin consciousness, and replace it with the righteousness consciousness described in Hebrews 9:14.

Righteousness by Faith

By definition, righteousness is the virtue of being completely justified, blameless, and totally accepted in God's sight. It is a state of being right with God. It comes from the Middle English word *rightwisnes*, which means "the character or quality of being right, a right-standing." As we all know, our righteousness before God is by faith in Christ alone. It is a free gift (Romans 5:17), totally unearned and not of our works, lest any man should boast. To help fashion this into a breastplate, the following series of Scriptures will draw a composite picture and framework for our understanding.

- The righteousness of God is to all and upon all that believe (Romans 3:22).
- Jesus has been made for us righteousness from God (1 Corinthians 1:30).
- Jesus was made sin with my sin so that I could be made righteous with His righteousness (2 Corinthians 5:21).
- Jesus took my place on the cross of God's judgment so that I could have a place with Him at the right hand of the Father. Righteousness is the supernatural grace and ability to stand before God as though sin had never existed in your life. Your sins are truly remembered no more. We have this right standing before the throne of God through the blood of Jesus (Hebrews 4:16; 10:19-22).

To deny our righteousness before God is to deny the blood of Christ that gave it to us. So, let's get back to our Scripture, Hebrews 9:14. How does this affect our conscience? The blood of Christ literally erases that old image of who we used to be and releases us to serve God in a new and living way. This totally releases us from our past (before God) and creates a new future where we serve God not out of guilt or remorse, but out of faith and love.

A Righteous Equation

First Thessalonians 5:8 describes our breastplate this way: "Put on the breastplate of faith and Love." *Faith plus love equals righteousness.* These are the two things given to us in the new birth. There is given to every one of us the measure of faith, and the love of God is shed abroad in our hearts by the Holy Spirit. These two together constitute our righteousness before God and are the foundation of our relationship with Him. To walk in this reality we must have a growing, unshakeable faith in God's passionate love for us and really see ourselves as totally righteous and accepted in His sight through the blood of Christ.

I exhort you to be unmovable on this! The total foundation for righteousness is through faith and love in the covenant sacrifice of Jesus and His death, burial, and resurrection. Our righteousness before God is not based on what we do in any way, shape, form, or fashion. It is based on what Jesus did, not what I do. This truth defends us from self-righteousness and self-condemnation. There is nothing I can do to make myself more acceptable to God than what Jesus has already done. *I must only believe.*

Freedom from Inferiority

The reality of righteousness delivers us and guards us against any feelings of inferiority. Inferiority is a most insidious and destructive attack of the enemy that has afflicted all of humanity since the garden of Eden. It was a major part of the strategy used against Eve in the garden. The reasoning of the serpent was designed to make Eve feel inferior and then cause her to believe that she could become superior by eating from the Tree of Knowledge of Good and Evil.

Feelings of inferiority are so destructive to our personal identity because it goes against everything we are called to become. Inferiority warps how we see ourselves and can cause self-doubt and even self-loathing. Our gifts and talents tend to become limited and neutralized by indecisiveness and the fear of failure. Worst of all is the internal pressure and turmoil it creates. Inferiority is the very antithesis of what we were created to be, and we will do almost anything to escape it. It is why Cain killed Abel. The underlying motivation in the first murder ever recorded in human history was caused by the feelings of inferiority that Cain felt "in God's presence." God had honored and received Abel's offering but refused Cain's. This refusal caused Cain's countenance and confidence to fall. His offering had been deemed inferior (in his mind) to Abel's offering. Even when God reasoned with Cain and shared the truth with him, it could not pierce the darkness that surrounded Cain's soul. The thought that his brother had made him look bad consumed his reasoning. So Cain rose up and killed his brother out of these feelings of inferiority and jealousy.

Here is truth. In the kingdom of God, no one is inferior to anyone else. We have all come into the kingdom the same way: by the King's love and grace. There is no striving or selfish ambition in an attempt to become greater or higher than someone else, because status in the kingdom is based on serving and promoting others. The very idea of having or wanting someone to be inferior to you is ridiculous in heaven's culture. Our God has given us all an equal and complete right standing before His throne; there is no competition with each other. No one can be more righteous than anyone else because the righteousness is a free gift to all who believe.

Unrighteousness

What happens to our breastplate if we go back to what we know is wrong and willfully sin? It is written that if we sin willfully, after we have received the knowledge of the truth, there remains no more sacrifice for our sin, but a certain fearful expectation of judgment. When we sin against what we know is true, our conscience condemns us. At this point, if we run to the Lord and do as instructed in 1 John 1:9—confess our sin and forsake it—He then is faithful and just to forgive us and cleanse us from all unrighteousness. At this point righteousness is restored in our souls, along with faith and confidence toward God. When Satan comes to attack us with condemnation and guilt for the sin, we can boldly tell him to shut up and leave—it's none of his business. If other people were involved we should tell them that we have confessed to the Lord and received His forgiveness. Now we are once again clothed with righteousness and delivered from a sin consciousness *in our souls*. These things are already and always true in our spirit. *The soul is the place of battle.*

If we continue in the sin, our conscience becomes defiled, and deliverance and restoration can become more difficult to obtain. Our souls become hardened through the deceit of sin, and the longer we continue, the greater the damage that must be restored. For those who have been in bondage a long time, it takes someone very skilled to deliver and restore them to a functional level of freedom. Even if the person has a really strong desire and commitment to be free it can still take a long time before they can walk with God on their own, which is always the goal in deliverance. But with God all things truly are possible!

The armor is even more critical for those who have been trapped in unrighteousness and have major issues. I have seen people in deep bondage begin to win victories very quickly once their souls were protected from further attack. The armor of God works for us no matter what condition we are in, because it is not our righteousness that makes it work, but His righteousness. It's not through our ability; it is through *His* ability. But we must desire it and we must believe it, because this is the crux of the issue. Do we desire to be free? Do we long to be delivered and walk with God? We know there is no limit to God's ability and power to restore us, but we will only be as free as we desire to be. I tell you the truth: if we desire freedom more than life itself, nothing can stop it. We should make it our goal to let everyone know that full freedom is available and attainable for all, no matter how strong the bondage. This hope and desire must burn bright in our hearts, as it will motivate us to attain liberty in every area of life.

Summary of the Breastplate of Righteousness

The breastplate protects the core of our being—*our new identities.*

- *Righteousness* comes from the Middle English word *rightwisnes*, the character or quality of being right.
- Righteousness is attained by faith alone. It is a free gift.
- It protects us from condemnation, self-righteousness, and feelings of inferiority.
- We are made righteous through the blood of Christ, not through works. This delivers us from a sin consciousness or any feelings of unworthiness.
- Righteousness is the combination of faith and love given to us in Christ.

Our Feet Shod with the Gospel of Peace

The word *feet* conveys the thought of direction and movement—where we are headed and what we are bringing there. *Feet* also speaks of purpose and intent, which implies *why* we are bringing something. A good illustration of this is a parallel Scripture to our text, found in Isaiah 52:7: "How beautiful on the mountains are the feet of him who brings good news, who proclaims peace." We are bringing good news. We are bringing these glad tidings to God's people for the purpose of proclamation. Our God reigns! He is the victor! He is the champion and has won our salvation! This is what we are carrying; this is what we are armed with. Wherever we go we are to be prepared with the good news of the peace that God has made available to us. Peace implies that the struggle is over; it is an end to the conflict. We have rest! Rest with whom? Rest with the world? No, we have rest with God! We now have peace with God through our Lord Jesus Christ. The whole world and most of the Church seems to think God is still mad at everyone and everything, but it is not so. Jesus literally died for the sins of the whole world; therefore, sin is no longer the problem. The real problem is that people don't know that the full price has been paid for them to be reconciled back to God and that all their sins can be totally eliminated if they will receive God's forgiveness, grace, and peace.

Understanding this ministry of reconciliation, which all believers have, is a big part of our preparation. This is described in 2 Corinthians 5:18-20. The conflict and inner turmoil in the lives of so many people will be eliminated when they are reconciled and have peace with God. The great grace of this piece of armor is that we are armed and prepared to be sent to bring reconciliation and peace. It implies a state of readiness to enter the conflicts of hurting, broken people with the good news of access to God's kingdom, where peace reigns. To be sure, this grace and peace has a time limit, and there is coming a day when God will judge the world through Jesus Christ. But for now it is grace and peace. Most of what is being called judgment now is only a matter of reaping what has been sown, combined with the attacks of the enemy.

Real Peace

Peace, in the Hebrew definition of the word, conveys the thought of wholeness, soundness, that all is well with us. The idea goes way beyond the thought that God is no longer mad at us and says that He is here to restore us and heal us, to make everything in our lives just as it should be. Naturally, the greatest example of this was Jesus, who came preaching peace and healing *all* who were oppressed of the Devil. We see Him healing the brokenhearted, giving sight to the blind and setting the captives free from the effects of sin. He was bringing them peace! This is our armor, our feet shod so that everywhere we go we are prepared to bring the good news that God's peace is available to all. *We are to be peacemakers!*

Influence

All of this has to do with our influence, which is a powerful force and must be protected. How we influence other people often has a ripple effect that reaches much farther that we realize. John the Baptist influenced the heart of the nation to turn back to God, preparing the way for the Messiah. After Jesus departed His disciples continued to influence Israel to be reconciled back to God. Ten years later, the good news of God's peace was extended to the Gentiles through Peter's anointed influence and obedience, and then by Paul to the regions beyond. We also see corrupt people using their influence to try to stop the gospel by stirring up the crowds with lies and false accusations. Be aware: Satan will constantly attempt to manipulate you and use your influence with people to promote his agenda.

So, to securely put on this piece of armor, we must ask ourselves what really influences us; how easily we are influenced; how prepared we are to influence our family, our community, our state, and our nation; and what direction we are trying to make everything go. Like Jesus and His disciples, we want to promote and project God's peace in the lives of everyone around us. This is a proper use of our influence.

As we do this, don't be surprised when the Devil tries to stir up bad influences against you, because peace is so destructive to the operations and schemes of the Devil. He is constantly seeking ways to destroy it. Satan's attacks are only fruitful in strife, confusion, divisions, and misunderstandings. This is why the apostle Paul said to mark those who cause division among us and avoid them. We are called to be peacemakers, not peacetakers!

Amazingly, it is this aspect of God's person working in our midst that totally crushes Satan and puts him under our *feet* (Romans16:20)!

Outline for Our Feet Shod with the Preparation of the Gospel of Peace

- Feet speak of direction—where we are headed and what we are bringing there.
- We need to be prepared with the good news of God's peace and of peace with God.
- This armor protects our influence, which must be guarded.

The Shield of Faith

[A]bove all taking the shield of faith
with which you shall be able to quench all the fiery
darts of the wicked one.
Ephesians 6:16

How important is it to have a big, stout shield in front of you when a volley of fire-tipped arrows are coming your way? The "above-all" importance of this piece of armor cannot be overstated, as it impacts the effectiveness of the rest of the armor. This "above all" designation lets us know that the shield of faith is to be functioning out in front of all the other pieces of armor; it is our first line of defense. This is also the first piece of armor designated by the word *taking*. As was mentioned, the first three pieces are designated as "having"—having our loins girt, having the breastplate on, and having our feet shod—which indicates that they are a constant, passive force and are foundational to our protection. The last three are designated by "taking," which indicates that they are to be actively operated in each attack or situation.

Operation

Concerning how it operates, the shield of faith is the bold, faith-filled declaration of the promises of God in direct response to whatever attacks are coming against us. Whether they are verbal attacks, the attitudes of people around us, adverse situations, or even dire circumstances, Satan will constantly seek ways to make them inflammatory in order to increase their destructive effect toward us. As believers we cannot keep quiet and just try to hold on. We must act! This action is speaking God's Word over our circumstances, especially if our circumstances are speaking to us. This shields our souls.

Our Lord Jesus said that if we would believe in Him the way Scripture says to, then out of our innermost being will flow rivers of living water. This flows out of us in the form of words—words of life and words of faith. The book of Proverbs reveals, "Council in the heart of a man is deep waters, and a wellspring of wisdom as a flowing brook." This living water, flowing out of our mouths and off of our lips will quench every fiery dart and will shield our souls from the barrages of doubt and unbelief that are being hurled against us.

Spirit of Faith

The shield of faith works in direct connection to the spirit of the faith that is in our hearts. "But since we have the same spirit of faith, according to what is written, 'I believe, therefore I spoke,' we also believe and therefore speak" (2 Corinthians 4:13). The spirit of faith doesn't consider the consequences or circumstances to be bigger than God, but simply declares God's unfailing promise. Our faith cannot be voiceless and still be effective. Proclamation equals power. There are two main hurdles that we must clear to move in this spirit of faith and activate the shield of faith. The first hurdle is a commitment to the process, or God's way of doing things—the way He has ordained for us to function.

Righteousness by Faith

The God-ordained process for His salvation working in us is to truly believe it in our hearts and say it with our mouths (Romans 10:9-10). This is the way we experience salvation. Now, here is the hurdle. Receiving our salvation is a one-time event, but working out our salvation is a process that takes a lifetime.

Here is the understanding. The way we receive salvation (hearing the Word, believing in it our hearts, and saying with our mouths) is the same way we work it out in every area of our lives; it is a lifelong process of growing up into Him in all things. When we believe and speak in agreement with what God has ordained for our lives, it activates the promises, and the Holy Spirit can work in us His good pleasure. Our faith is supposed to grow (2 Thessalonians 1:3). When faith stops growing, it starts dying. It must continue to grow. God has ordained that the just shall live by faith.

How does faith continue to grow? Faith comes by hearing, and it grows by saying and doing what we hear and believe in our hearts. As we continue in this process, our faith becomes a *giant, powerful shield,* able to effectively stop the barbs of accusation that Satan is constantly seeking to wound us with. This process is the right way to our victory—it is righteousness by faith.

Know the Promises

The second main hurdle is to know and embrace the promises. These great and precious promises have been given to us to call us out of the world and into the inheritance that God has prepared for us. Our faith doesn't work just because we believe something; it doesn't work just because we speak it. It works because we believe and speak what God has promised to perform in our lives. Every promise has in it the power to bring it to pass, and God watches over His Word to perform it. Like Abraham, we cannot waver at God's promises to us, but must be fully convinced that He will perform them as we enter in and boldly proclaim His Word. This takes knowledge. Take time to become intimately aware of what God has revealed concerning His will for the major areas of your life. Have fellowship with the Lord over these promises. Discuss them with Him in prayer and let Him show you a land flowing with milk and honey.

A Defense

When in operation, the shield of faith defends us from the ungodly forces of fear, doubt, and unbelief. These forces are constantly seeking to gain access to our souls and penetrate our hearts to rob us of our hope in God's promises. For example, a new believer is enjoying his newfound faith and is walking with God and growing, when suddenly he gets hit with temptation and an old sin trips him up. In his heart he knew better, and now he feels like he failed God. Then comes the Enemy's lies as he accuses God and the new believer, saying, "You blew it. You knew better. God can't forgive that." This works with a lot of new believers because they don't know better; they are unarmed and vulnerable. Then someone shows the new believer 1 John 1:9 and explains how God promised that they can be cleansed from any unrighteousness if they confess and forsake it. Now faith comes anew and they receive forgiveness, so when the enemy attacks them with "You blew it; you are a hypocrite," the believer responds with "Devil, you are a liar. The blood of Jesus cleansed me of that, and God loves me!" This battle is won! The shield of faith quenched those fiery darts.

Here is another example. Currently much of the United States is experiencing a recession. Everyone around you starts saying how bad it is, and then here comes the attack of the Enemy against your mind, trying to steal your peace. The Devil hits you with thoughts like "What are you going to do now? What if you lose your job, your house? What are you going to do?!" The spirit of faith responds, "I know what we are going to do! We are going to stand fast on God's Word, which says, 'I have never seen the righteous forsaken or his seed begging bread.' My God will guide me. God will give me wisdom and keep me safe. Devil, you are a liar."

As we declare His Word, faith comes flooding out of our hearts, the shield goes up around our souls, and all of those fiery darts of doubt and worry are quenched. Some say, "Yeah, but what if the darts are still coming? What if I am getting ready for bed, but the thoughts are still burning in my brain—'What are we going to do now?'" Keep saying the Word; keep declaring the promises. Take your stand and say it again and again, until the fires are put out. If your house was on fire would you want the firemen to put a little water on it, or pour it on until the fire is completely out? After you take your stand on the Word, then take time to listen to what the Spirit of God has to say. His Words will lead you to peace and victory.

Outline for the Shield of Faith:

- Above all, take the shield.
- It is the bold declaration of God's promise over our circumstances.
- It works in conjunction with the spirit of faith; proclamation equals power.
- It defends against the ungodly forces of fear, doubt, and unbelief.

The Helmet

The salvation spoken of here is not primarily the salvation we received at conversion when we made Jesus our Lord, but rather the physical and mental salvation we currently need in our present circumstances and situations.

As we have seen in Isaiah 59:17, Jesus Himself put on this helmet of salvation while He was here on earth, not because He needed to be saved from sin, but because He armed Himself to do His Father's will in the midst of a sinful, dangerous world. The actual function and working of the helmet is more fully expressed in 1 Thessalonians 5:8, which calls our helmet "the hope of salvation." In every conflict there must be a clear hope of victory and deliverance. We need a hope that sees beyond our present condition by fixing our eyes on Jesus and the fulfillment of our Father's goodwill and pleasure in our situation (Psalm 27:13). This is imparted through knowing and believing the promises God has given us for overcoming every attack of the enemy. For instance, our Father promised us in 1 Corinthians 10:13 that He is faithful and will make a way for us to escape any and every temptation we are facing. There is a way! If there was no way out, then the situation would be hopeless, but we have real hope, because we know through Him that it is possible to overcome every temptation. Jesus is our hope. He defeated death, hell, and the grave. While He was here on earth He defeated every temptation and overcame every obstacle, and now promises to help us walk in that same victory.

This is good news! This is the gospel of our salvation. God has empowered us to walk free from anything that would try to hold us back or keep us bound. It is the power to change our thoughts, our habits, and the circumstances of our lives. God's grace and power working in us can turn any hopeless situation around and fill it with Him. Romans 15:13 reveals that the God of hope will cause us to abound in hope through the power of the Holy Spirit. This is our helmet. It defends us from discouragement and despair.

When the situations that we are up against seem too big for us, and from a natural standpoint some disaster seems imminent, our souls are protected with the knowledge that He is the God of our salvation and nothing can snatch us out of His hand. We are truly kept by the power of God through faith unto a full salvation, spirit, soul, and body.

The Source

> My soul faints for your salvation,
> but I hope in your Word.
> Psalm 119:81

Once again, the source of our hope is God's unchanging promises, but even more than that, our God swore an oath to us in Hebrews 6:13-19 that He would perform these promises without fail. He swore this oath upon Himself, meaning that if he fails to keep His promise, then He will cease to be. God did this so that we might have a strong, unwavering consolation in this world. His promises to us are sure and steadfast. This hope acts as an anchor to our souls and will keep us from drifting off into uncertainty and doubt during *any* storm. Our hope has the ability to transcend all earthly situations and reach into the very presence of God within the veil, where Jesus abides. He is our hope, and we believe that where He is, we will be also. Every victory He won will be ours as well. Everything He inherited as the beloved Son of God we will also inherit, even to the point that as He is, so shall we be in this world. This hope purifies our thoughts, our choices, and our emotional responses toward life.

Why?

Hope is always future tense (Romans 8:24). It is a confident, eager expectation of things to come that is created in us by seeing God's plan for us. This is not a worldly hope, like "I hope so" or "maybe so." Our hope is full of the assurance that we need (Hebrews 6:9-11). It seems that our heavenly Father has gone to extraordinary lengths to give us an unquenchable hope.

This prompts a few questions. Why is hope so necessary to the human soul? Why does the expectation of future events so powerfully affect our present reality? I am sure a large part of it is because we know in our hearts that we were created for greater things. So much of what we are meant to be was lost in the fall of mankind, and we have been seeking it ever since. Romans 8:20 states how the whole of creation was unwillingly subjected to the futility of such a limited existence and is eagerly waiting for the reality of our true destiny.

For this purpose the Son of God was revealed, and He has filled our future with the glorious hope of recovering *all* that was lost to us, and much more! So, armed with this understanding we will not be so vulnerable to the discouragement and despair that the enemy attacks us with. Through the Word of God our souls are being filled with visions of a glorious future that empowers us to see beyond our present. This future has far more power to affect our lives right now than any past or present condition does. We will be able to respond to the adverse situations around us from an eternal, supernatural perspective.

I have found that there are four baseline responses to these adverse conditions of life that are common to everyone.

1. Ignore them. Presently, we are finite beings and have a limited amount of time and attention. If we tried to respond to everything going on around us daily it would drive us to distraction. So we naturally begin to categorize the importance of things around us and decide what needs our attention. The rest we ignore.

2. Struggle with them. Sometimes we find it difficult to decide what needs our attention and what is a distraction. This indecision creates unresolved issues, which build up over time and cause us to struggle. Sometimes the struggle is simply knowing what we should do but not really wanting to do it.

3. Accept them. This is a most difficult response to change and overcome. When we accept limitations or negative situations as the boundaries for our lives, then we lose the power to move beyond them. We must allow the Lord to determine for us what is acceptable.

4. Change them. This is the one response that takes the power of God. The power and capacity for positive change is released in us as we behold our calling and destiny revealed in the Word. The decision to change activates hope and guards us from any discouragement in our present condition or situation.

So, when the storms of life come, let's be like Peter and fix our eyes on Jesus, the author and perfector of our faith. As we consider Him and all that He endured to bring us so great a salvation, we will not grow weary and faint in our minds on the day of battle.

Outline of the Helmet of Salvation:

- Our helmet is the hope of salvation, physical, mental, and spiritual.
- Hope sees beyond the present situation to God's promised salvation.
- Hope is an anchor. It focuses our thoughts on the outcome of the Word.
- The helmet defends against discouragement, despair, and hopelessness.

Sword of the Spirit

And the Sword of the Spirit, which is the Word of God
Ephesians 6:17

This sword is the great offensive weapon of our arsenal. Our enemies have no armor, shield, or defense against it. Throughout Scripture the sword is an instrument of judgment and war. In this case it is arming us to execute and enforce the will of our King, Jesus. This truth is beautifully displayed in Psalm 149, where it says, "Let the high praises of God be in their mouth, and a two-edged sword in their hand, to execute on them the written judgment. This honor have all the saints!"

The other five pieces of armor are mostly defensive and protective in operation, but the sword is our God-given ability to retaliate against the attack of the enemy and begin to take an offensive position, which is vital to our being victorious. You can't win battles by simply having a good defense; the defensive armor is given to protect us *while* we are attacking and destroying every stronghold of the enemy. If we limit ourselves to only operating defensively, it will create an attitude of survival Christianity, which has permeated the church for far too long. Those trapped in survival Christianity quickly develop a victim mentality that makes them feel as though they have no control over their circumstances. This has a devastating effect on our faith and prayer focus; we will spend most of our prayer time telling God about everything that is happening to us that we don't like, hoping that something will change. The offensive operation of the sword of the Spirit changes all that and empowers us to attack our enemy and our circumstances with authority.

Rhema

Logos and *rhema* are the two words in the Greek new testament text that are translated as *word* when referring to the Word of God. *Logos* represents the Word in its entirety, both the Living Word, Jesus ("The Logos was with God and the Logos was God" (John 1:1)), and the written Word ("rightly dividing the Logos of truth" (2 Timothy 2:15)). *Rhema* represents the specific Word spoken to us ("but every rhema that proceeds out of the mouth of God," (Matthew 4:4); "nevertheless, at your rhema I will let down the net"(Luke 5:5)).

The sword of the Spirit is the "rhema" of God. In order to deal with the attacks and situations we are up against, the Holy Spirit will lead us to specific scriptures in the (Logos) Word of God for empowerment and activation. Then as the Holy Spirit speaks these specific Words and reveals them to us, they create faith ("faith comes by hearing, and hearing by the rhema of God" (Romans 10:17)) in our hearts and release glorious power in us. We then take these faith-filled Scriptures that the Holy Spirit has given us and pray, declaring these promises boldly before the throne of God, to obtain mercy and receive grace to help us in our time of need.

Then we declare these promises over our situation and release them in the spirit, thereby releasing the power and blessing of God over our lives and situations. (This activates angelic activity.)

Then we declare them to the principalities and powers for judgment and execution of the actions that they have taken against us, thereby binding them and casting them down. Now all of the defensive armor kicks in as we determine to walk in and obey this rhema Word until the Enemy is completely destroyed and the victory is obtained.

This is the sword of the Spirit in operation: faith-producing, power-filled words from God given to us under the inspiration and anointing of the Holy Spirit for the purpose of revealing and proclaiming the will of our Father and destroying the works of the enemy. When we go on the offense like this, we really do some damage to the kingdom of darkness. The principalities and powers have no defense whatsoever against the sword of the spirit; it devastates them. They can only hope that you don't find out about it and have the will and desire to implement it. Too late!

Now, once we get armed and begin to win victories over the attacks of the enemy, the Lord will lead us into Ephesians 6:18. After we become proficient at receiving the rhema Word from God for ourselves, the Lord will allow us to help bring victory to our brothers and sisters by praying with the rhema Word over their life. It really gets to be enjoyable when our victory becomes victory for others.

Armed for Intercession

This is the great purpose and overall strategy of the armor: being equipped for intercession. True intercession is the combination of prayer and action necessary to bring deliverance. This was the reason our great intercessor Jesus put it on—so that He might intercede in the affairs of man to bring God's justice and righteousness to all. Once we are armed we are called into the prayer ministry with Jesus and admonished to pray always with all manner of prayer and supplication in the spirit with all perseverance and supplication for all saints (Ephesians 6:18). The tremendous blessing of this armor must go beyond just our personal benefit to remain effective.

Chapter 5

Anointed Spiritual Warfare

DUE TO THE FACT THAT the term "spiritual warfare" means so many different things to different people, I state up front that the only true and effective basis for dealing with this subject is the Word of God. No matter what our experiences have been (good or bad), we must be willing to examine them and gain understanding from our experiences based on what God has already revealed in Scripture.

Our warfare has many expressions, yet one singular purpose: to see Christ formed in us. This eternal purpose, which was given to us in Christ Jesus before time began, is our destiny and calling. All of the spiritual activities that we are involved in—the gifts of the Holy Spirit, the fruit of the spirit, prayer, worship, giving, and so on—are all working together to conform us into the image of His dear Son, in whom we have this redemption (Romans 8:26-30).

This is what the intercession of the Holy Spirit is bringing us into. This was the focus and travail of the apostle Paul's intercession for the Galatian church, that Christ would be formed in them. Anything else is falling short of our purpose.

Spirit Anointed

Anointed spiritual warfare is the focused, Holy-Spirit-led application of the Word of God that produces lasting results. I have witnessed some yelling matches where people screamed at demons for an hour but weren't very anointed and didn't produce any real results. There may be times when we raise our voice in exercising our authority over demonic spirits, but being loud isn't what makes it work. Faith in God and being anointed makes it work. We know how God anointed Jesus of Nazareth with the Holy Spirit and with power, and He then went about doing good and healing all who were oppressed by the Devil, because God was with Him.

Sometimes He got loud, and sometimes He did it in a quiet corner, but the bottom line is that it was always effective. This is our desire: for the entire body of Christ to be effective in our warfare. As we learn to skillfully use the weapons of our warfare, every stronghold of the Enemy will fall before us. Take a look at 2 Corinthians 10:3-6 for an anointed (Spirit-empowered) focus and battle plan.

Go to War

To begin with, we do not war according to the flesh or by using any worldly motives or methods. We are not doing this to look spiritual or try to prove anything. We are not going to operate in earthly wisdom or willpower to make something happen. True spiritual power and authority are the only things that will prevail here, not carnal machinations. Verse four says they are the weapons (armor) of *our* warfare. This warfare is not something we ask God to do. Not one time in the entire New Testament does God ever promise to take authority over the Devil for us. God has done all He is going to do about Satan, until the end of time. He said, "You resist the Devil, and he will flee from you."

Through His death, burial, and resurrection, Jesus completely defeated the entire kingdom of darkness—for you! He already had complete authority and power over Satan and every demonic spirit and work. All that Jesus did on the earth He did for us, so that we could be just as free and victorious as He was.

In the great intercessory prayer of Ephesians 1, Paul, through the Holy Spirit, prayed that we the believers would know the exceeding greatness of His power, the same power that He wrought in Christ when God raised Him from the dead (the lowest place) and seated Him at His own right hand in the heavenly places (the highest place), *far* above every principality, power, might, and dominion and every name that is named, not only in this present world, but also the world to come. He put *all* these things under His feet. If you are in the body of Christ, it has *all* been put under your feet also, because we have been raised up together and been made to sit together *with Him* in these heavenly places of spiritual authority.

Warfare is not something we ask God to do for us. It is what we must do by His grace and power. These weapons of our warfare are mighty and effective through God. God is Spirit; therefore, these things must be done in the Spirit, by the Spirit, and through the Spirit. They are mighty for pulling down strongholds, a stronghold being a concept or pattern of thought that defends or justifies anything in your life as being acceptable when it is contrary to God's Word. If we are going to be effective in pulling down these strongholds in our souls, it is necessary that we be totally honest and open with the Holy Spirit and willing to examine what we believe in the light of truth. We must love the truth more than our own lives. I have seen so many people try to justify what they think by claiming that they have the right to believe whatever they want to believe. If Jesus is our Lord, that thought is a lie! We gave up the right to believe whatever we think and traded it in for God's truth. Now we seek to know and believe what God thinks about everything, because we know He is always right.

We are casting down imaginations and anything that would try to exalt itself over the true knowledge of who God really is and what He is like. Since most people really don't know God in His Word, they have to rely on their imaginations to create their own concepts of Him, which usually ends up really distorted. Paul feared that something like this might happen to the church at Corinth—that somehow, just as the serpent deceived Eve by his craftiness, their minds might be corrupted from simple obedience to Christ. Eve's instructions were simple: don't eat of the tree. The serpent began to reason with her and to explain that her situation wasn't that simple. He declared to her a different outcome than the one she was told and gave Eve a different reason and motive for the instruction that she was given. The serpent stated that she would not die, and that God told her that because He knew something that He didn't want Eve to know. The serpent was saying, "God deceived you." In order for this deception to work, he had to attack God's integrity and corrupt Eve's inner image of what God was really like, because as long as Eve trusted God and believed His Word, Satan's deception had no place in her. So, how did Eve respond? She thought about what the serpent said and decided to find out for herself.

Here is the point: these imaginations and reasonings that exalt themselves against the true knowledge of God in our minds must be cast down, not *thought out*. We are to take our spiritual weapons and totally destroy every lie and deception of the Enemy of our souls.

Noemata

This is a very important and interesting word in the Greek text that will help our understanding of what our enemy is trying to accomplish: *noemata*. *Noemata* is one of those "hidden" words that is translated several different ways but still has the same basic idea. In our text it is used in the singular form, *noema*: "bringing every thought [noema] captive" (2 Corinthians 10:5). This is not speaking of every single thought that comes into our head, but rather every conclusion or pattern of thought. It is first used in 2 Corinthians 2:11: "lest Satan should take advantage of us, for we are not ignorant of his devices [noemata]." The context for this statement is forgiveness. Paul said in the proceeding verse, "Whom you forgive anything, I also forgive." He did not want Satan to get a foothold in the church there at Corinth through unforgiveness, a very common and effective device of the enemy. This brings up a question: what are the patterns of thought that lead to unforgiveness? We have all heard them plenty of times—statements like "Did you here what they said to you? They can't talk to you like that" or "Look at what they did to you. You don't have to put up with that" or a real favorite of Satan: "Why did God let this happen to you? Doesn't He care?" All of this is designed by the enemy to cause strife and unforgiveness to destroy relationships. These are the "wiles" of the Devil that we are told to stand against.

Patterns of Thought

The Holy Spirit wants to help us identify and cast down these satanically induced thought patterns that constantly give Satan an advantage over us. One of the indicators that will help us identify these areas is examining the fruit. Jesus said, "You will know them by their friut." The same is true of thought patterns; fruit doesn't lie. Someone may call the tree in his or her front yard a peach tree, but if I see apples all over it every year, it's an apple tree. If we have areas in our lives that are bearing bad fruit, we must ask the Holy Spirit for light in those areas. Then we must allow Him to renew our thinking about that area as we attack it with the weapons of our warfare. Having light in all the areas of our live is a *big* issue.

We see another startling use of the word *noemata* in 2 Corinthians 4:4: ". . . whose minds [noemata, pattern of thinking] the god of this age has blinded, who do not believe, lest the light should shine to them." This is speaking, of course, of unbelievers, yet there is still application to us who believe. Even after we receive the light of salvation in our hearts, we still have a lot of problems with our heads. Many of the old patterns of thinking still remain and must be systematically replaced, which is actually another way of saying that we must have our minds renewed, but with a specific focus. There are old thought patterns that are so ingrained into our thinking that they keep the light of God from shining into areas of our souls. These become the strongholds of the enemy.

Be ready

> . . . and being ready to punish all disobedience
> when your obedience is fulfilled.
> 2 Corinthians 10:6

When the light of God's Word breaks through into our souls and we pull down a stronghold in some area of our lives, then we are able to help someone else get victory in the same area. Getting victory over one thing doesn't mean you have victory over everything. There are still many battles to fight and win, and we can only give to others what has been manifested in our own lives. To try to do otherwise, no matter how good our intentions are, will only make the situation worse. Many times people think that they have heard from God because they clearly see the problem, but it's not so.

Here is wisdom: we have heard from God when we see His answer to the problem, not just the problem itself. A graphic example of this is the seven sons of Sceva. They saw Paul successfully casting out evil spirits, so, being Jewish exorcists, they tried to do what Paul did. They found someone to minister to and rightly knew what the person's problem was, but they didn't personally know the answer, Jesus, like Paul did. So when the seven sons of Sceva tried to use Paul's answer to cast out the demon, they ended up wounded and naked.

Make sure your obedience is fulfilled and your victory is secure before you try to attack areas of disobedience in someone else. Before you give someone advice about relationships, examine your own thoughts about relationships, in light of God's Word, and then share with them in the areas where you have been successful. On the other hand, when you are receiving advice or ministry, make sure that person's life demonstrates the victory you want to see in your own life. Generally speaking, it would be foolish to think someone else's advice or prayers are going to do more for you than they do for them. Look for qualified ministry with a proven track record of personal victory. I say "generally speaking" because through the gifts of the Holy Spirit people can minister and impart victory beyond what they have personally attained. Be led by the Spirit!

Chapter 6

David's Armor

THE STORY OF DAVID AND Goliath in 1 Samuel 17 challenges us to live and believe beyond our natural limitations. The life of David is such an exquisite portrait of what it is to be a man after God's own heart. The combination of fearlessness and meekness that he demonstrated is so compelling that it draws us into being wholehearted men and women of God and awakens in us a desire to be a champion for Him. As we examine the armor of God working in David's soul in his triumph over Goliath, I pray that you will be filled with visions of glorious victory over every enemy you face, through our Lord Jesus Christ.

Goliath defied and taunted the armies of Israel. When the men of Israel heard of the defiance, they felt dismay and great fear. When the men of Israel saw Goliath they fled from him and were dreadfully afraid. How could this be? Israel had a glorious covenant with the almighty God of heaven and earth—a covenant that had been proven faithful time and time again by giving them victory over every enemy. How could one loudmouthed pagan put such fear into the hearts of these men? David heard and saw the same giant (1 Samuel 17:23), and it made him indignant. His thought was "Who does this philistine think he is?" Then, when David heard about the reward that anyone would receive if they killed Goliath, he began to view the giant as an awesome opportunity.

The Truth

Why was the response of David's heart so different from the rest of the men of Israel? The loins of his mind were girded with the truth and reality of his covenant with the Most High God. He believed it. He had heard the accounts of Abraham and his household servants, who defeated the armies of the five kings; of Caleb, who took a whole mountain full of giants and defeated them; and of Joshua, who defeated whole nations as they entered their promised land. In David's eyes, his God was far bigger than this problem. Therefore, Goliath was dead meat, because he had defied the armies of the *living* God. Dead gods can't do a whole lot for you, but with the living God, all things are possible to those who believe. The same is true in us today. Does not our covenant say "But thanks be to God, who gives us the victory through our Lord Jesus Christ," and "Now thanks be to God, who always leads us in triumph in Christ"? Is there not a cause?

Oh, Brother

As David began to speak his confidence in God, his older brother mistook it for cockiness. Eliab got upset and began to downplay his little brother. He was going to put him in his place. But David already knew his place, and he answered, "Is there not a cause?" He was saying, "This loudmouthed giant came out and challenged the living God, and as a man of Israel in covenant with God, I have a right to respond to that challenge."

Be prepared for this! When you step out in faith and display your spiritual armor, some of your brothers and sisters will get upset, because they will perceive you as being proud and your faith will confront their fears and unbelief. When this happens, be gracious, be patient, and be kind. Continue to walk in love and remember that you are fighting for their victory also. As you begin to knock down giants, they will come around to the truth and get excited about winning some victories as well.

Good News

It came to Saul's attention that there was someone in the camp who wasn't afraid of Goliath, so he immediately latched on to this glimmer of hope and sent for him. David brought Saul the good news: "Let no man's heart fail because of him; your servant will go and fight with this philistine." Because David's mind was girded with the truth, he could see himself as a giant killer. David concluded that he and God were more than enough to get the job done. Being armed with this truth empowered David to bring the gospel of peace to Israel. He was telling Saul, "Don't be afraid. Be at peace. We can beat this." David's feet were shod with the good news—*our God reigns!*

Breastplate

When Saul saw David, his heart sank, and he said, "You are not able." Saul was viewing him from a natural standpoint, of course, but David knew who he was in God. He had on his breastplate of righteousness and began testifying to Saul about his relationship with God as a deliverer. He said, "Your servant has killed both lion and bear; and this uncircumcised philistine will be like one of them, seeing he has defied the armies of the living God."

Seeing! *Seeing!* This is the vital point. David saw the whole army this way, but the army didn't. None of the soldiers of Israel had on their breastplates. Being clothed with our new identities in Christ keeps us in a position to see the world around us from a heavenly perspective. It is a breastplate of faith and love—loving God for who He is to us and all that He has done for us, and faith in God that we are to Him all that He says we are, and that through Him we can do all that He says for us to do. David's soul was filled with this reality!

A Helmet

"Moreover David said, 'The Lord who delivered me from the paw of the lion and from the paw of the bear, HE will deliver me from the hand of this Philistine'" (1 Samuel 17:37). He knew *who* his salvation was. David already had a clear hope and vision of God delivering him in this situation. It was a hope that stayed with him through many trials all the days of his life.

> David declared this hope in God over and over in the Psalms: Let them be confounded and consumed who are the adversaries of my life; Let them be covered with reproach and dishonor who seek my hurt. But I will hope continually, and will praise you yet more and more. (Psalm 71:13-14)

Let us also rejoice in hope and refuse discouragement and doubt.

Not Natural

Saul decided to let David fight and was going to help him out by letting David use his own personal armor, but it didn't take David very long to realize that Saul's armor wasn't going to work. He knew his salvation and victory was not going to come through any natural means.

We must come to the same conclusion in our warfare and be very judicious about what we put our trust in. There are so many self-help books and so much man-centered psychology floating around in the church that it causes people to rely on natural means for gaining victory over their life situations. We don't need behavior modification. *We need deliverance!*

Here is the truth: whatever you presently have in your hand, plus faith in God and obedience to the leading of the Holy Spirit, is enough to win in your current situation. If there is something else you need to complete your victory, God will lead you to it. David had a staff in his hand, his shepherd's pouch, and his sling. On his way to the giant, he stopped at a brook, chose five smooth, well-worn stones, and was now fully equipped for giant hunting. This is our cue!

Five is the number of grace (grace, by definition, is God's supernatural empowerment to do His will), so we go to God's Word and pick our five smooth, well-worn revelations of God's victory working in our lives, put them in our pouches (minds), and get ready to attack. You will probably only need one word from God to take out your giant, but it is always good to have more than enough.

A Shield

"But You, O Lord are a shield for me, my glory and the One who lifts my head" (Psalm 3:3). As David drew near, the Philistine began to curse him by his gods, and said, "Come to me, and I will give your flesh to the birds of the air and the beasts of the field." But you can't curse what God has blessed, so Goliath's curse had to return on his own head. David's response to these fiery darts was his shield: "You come at me with a sword, with a spear, and with a javelin. But I come at you in the name of the Lord of Hosts, the God of the armies of Israel, whom you have defied." (1 Samuel 17:45). When he declared this, David's faith in his God *nullified* any of the intended effects of the curses and threats of his enemy. Those same curses would have had a devastating effect on any other man in Israel's entire army if he had to face that giant, even though they were the army of the living God.

Why? Why would these threats affect every other man in Israel except David? David's *soul* was armed with a *reality* that far exceeded this situation! He didn't care what Goliath said or what weapons he had to attack him with, because it couldn't match what God had, and it didn't change who God was in David's eyes. In the face of the whole situation he could still boldly say, "The Lord is my light and my salvation; whom shall I fear? The Lord is the strength of my life; of whom shall I be afraid?" God can only be to us what we say He is. If we say He is our Lord and Savior, then He can save us. If we boldly declare Him to be our deliverer, He will deliver us. If we keep silent, only our Enemy's voice will be heard.

The Sword

David prophesied to that giant by the Word of the Lord,

> This day the Lord will deliver you into my hand, and I will strike you and take your head from you. And this day I will give the carcasses of the camp of the Philistines to the birds of the air and to the wild beasts of the earth, that all the earth may know that there is a God in Israel.

Then he ran toward their whole army to meet that Philistine (faith runs at problems). Once the Word of the Lord goes forth, there is no retreat. We pursue our enemies until they are destroyed and the Word is fulfilled!

When you have your enemy on the ground, cut off its head. The head represents authority, and while we are in a position of victory, we want to be thorough in cutting off anything in our lives that would give this Enemy authority to trouble us again. Bringing everything in our lives into a full submission to the lordship of Jesus is always the ultimate place of victory and safety.

The Father said to Jesus, "Sit at my right hand, Till I make your enemies your footstool." We know Jesus must reign from there until He has put all enemies under His feet, and I count it a glorious honor to be a part of God's end-time army and to be involved in fulfilling this decree.

> "Now thanks be to God who always leads us in triumph in Christ, and through us diffuses the fragrance of His knowledge in every place."

Made in the USA
Middletown, DE
11 February 2022

60969198R00050